Several Forms of Speech
New, Early, Escaped and Last Poems

Several Forms of Speech
New, Early, Escaped and Last Poems
Arnold Rattenbury

Published 2008 by
Smokestack Books
PO Box 408, Middlesbrough TS5 6WA
e-mail : info@smokestack-books.co.uk
www.smokestack-books.co.uk

Several Forms of Speech
New, Early, Escaped and Last Poems
Arnold Rattenbury
Copyright 2008 Sim Rattenbury, all rights reserved

Cover: detail from Mummer's shirt, Costume Museum, Nottingham

Printed by
EPW Print & Design Ltd

ISBN 978-0-9548691-82
Smokestack Books gratefully
acknowledges the support of
Middlesbrough Borough Council
and Arts Council North East

Smokestack Books is a member of
Independent Northern Publishers
www.northernpublishers.co.uk
and is represented by Inpress Ltd
www.inpressbooks.co.uk

Contents

New
- 9 Twitching
- 10 Waiting with Sim
- 11 The Communist
- 14 *from* Going and Coming
    2: The Bog-Oak Dragons
- 15 3: Clown
- 16 4: Three Prentice Pieces
- 17 5: The Hirwaun and Treforest Steelworker Portraits, c 1835
- 18 7: The Last Wakes Week Train, Rhyl, 1970s
- 19 8: PJ de Loutherbourg, 1740-1812, arr. London '71

Early
- 20 The Bishop's Prologue
- 22 Song before Embarkation, 1943
- 23 Incident in Training
- 24 Calendar Song

Escaped
- 25 'Then, by inspiration'
- 26 Late Bermudas
- 28 Preparing for Bed after Reading Pope
- 29 Snow in the Early Morning at Putney
- 31 Another Four Characters
    1: Tripper, Harlech
- 32 2: Girl in a Yellow Sack
- 33 3: Church Dignitary
- 34 4: Commuter
- 35 The Loss of View from Hafodty
- 36 Flask
- 37 Lines on a Ladies Magazine Feature
- 38 Bee Notions
- 40 Chapter Four
- 44 Sunday in August 1968
- 45 Calculated Acts
- 46 Waiting for the Revolution by Siop Parry
- 47 The Migneint, with an Image of Christ

Last
48 Ysbyty Goffa

53 A Note on the Text

55 Notes

'In this book a number of dialects are used, to wit: the Missouri negro dialect; the extremist form of the backwoods South-Western dialect; the ordinary 'Pike-County' dialect; and four modified versions of this last. The shadings have not been done in a haphazard fashion, or by guess-work; but PAINSTAKINGLY, AND WITH THE TRUSTWORTHY GUIDANCE AND SUPPORT OF PERSONAL FAMILIARITY WTH THESE SEVERAL FORMS OF SPEECH.

I make this explanation for the reason that without it many readers would suppose that all these characters were trying to talk alike and not succeeding.'

(Mark Twain, *Huckleberry Finn*)

Twitching

Fantastic! And all written with a feather!
(Sam Goldwyn on Shakespeare)

Proof of punning, nuthatches go
quite nutty for Sim's bird-nut feeder -
Three, four, five at a time, the greedy
buggers. Proof of rhythm,
the way they make it swing for them,
then hop to look-out points, measure for measure.

Rhymes at need exactly fit each
character's provenance, just as their ditties
prove the birdbook fight - by yelps
and postman whistlings, trills, god-help-us
noddings (or so they write of spring)
Between each fit of the breed's love-sing.

Proof of image? Well, say
The abruptness of these lines, then a getaway.

Waiting with Sim

Sometimes the world hangs dumb, but never
is. Today soft rain dithers,
sways up the *traeth* towards us; then,
from motionless as a pall, slithers
up-mountain or back to the *traeth* again
Barely movement - or even, purposely, weather.

Yet out in this shilly-shally we must.
Droplets making it up reveal
themselves: a population of air
various as might be kinds of people -
sopping, pearl-like, according to where
you look from - all for the present quite lost.

Life gets weathered though, to go
ahead. Out in it so long together, we know.

The Communist

*six sonnets jostling a seventh, regarding a fine Welsh painting
of the 1930s ,'The Communist' by Evan Walters*

> How far down have the lies rooted
> themselves and blossomed and borne fruit?

Inside the frame men and women
seem about equal, in number at least -
though here it's He stands out from the crowd:
on that soapbox, She would too
of course. The rest, listening, shadow
each other, grey by comparison.
Indoors would show a similar huddle
awkward on kitchen chairs, sunk
into front-room cushions, cold on an institute's
bentwood. If we must generalise -
and all the lies are general -
all that distinguishes Him or Her
is being speaker while the others listen.
That is, any is one of us.

> So widespread grow the weeds and thick
> the choke that old intention sickens.

Who we were, who we were not
still seems important. Mostly, workfolk
whose cause was ours met in the workplace,
even their meetings a kind of lock-in.
Call us the others dissatisfied
therefore: housewife, doleman, artist,
apprentice, the blocked from vision who knew
in our bones, our shadows, that same grey matter,
things would not gradually come better
but of a sudden, by violence
if needs must, as times before us,
workplace or here, came leaping their bounds.
Thinking as we did then, face
privilege and outface kings, even
beheading one…

> Or has the soil become exhausted
> Beyond the point that things be forced?

> Beyond this painted

corner, we had combined, entered
history, voted, moved beyond countries,
struck out, stopped whole systems. And when
great slaughters engulfed the world, you must
see war itself engulfed by us;
nations furious that change themselves,
ourselves included. And we, the dead
and maimed and killers and living present
to prove it. You've heard the lies that prime
and beefy generals and ministers
did the world. Forget that nonsense.
Except in fiasco, effort and reason
came from here, out of these shadows.

> Pale, the few seedlings bend swaying
> and sometimes squabble in each other's way.

Routes to that street-corner
matter - most words offer a pun,
so how we came to be rooted there,
listening, will do. By catchword? Slogan?
sales pitch it didn't work like that
though labels abounded - foreign phrases
from other towns and countries doing
what we did. Sang their songs sometimes,
would fight beside them once, before
that great engulfing war - towards
its prevention. But in the end, in the local,
only a mother and father tongue
made sense of self. Dialect
not jargon told us the way to go.

> Crop-spray, much like baton-charge
> or tannoy, poisons the air's largeness.

And so the painting shows a crowd
outside a lockout? Pit head disaster?
Imminent closure? Those - a Him
or Her - this side of the slam-shut gates,
are poor and wanting. So where's the difference?
Whose sweat does the profit rise from?
Who needs war for the prop and never
mind the slaughter? All right, profits
increase. At whose expense? You see
how hard it is to see how hard
you find the picture's commonsense?
No-one could paint it now - only
because, though the grey grey matters remain,
who can get up and speak for us?

> What would Then say Now, nosing
> about to watch how its garden grows?

Now at His peroration, arms
flung out, face up to the clouds,
shut-eyed, on tiptoe, straining for take-off:
some have called him cruciform,
the moment religious, his red shirt bloody
with sacrifice. There were indeed
bibliomantics among us, chapter
and verse at the ready, shrines abroad.
But cruciform? To us he's more
the athlete breasting a tape, or lover
arms outstretched in welcome so
that his love will come in here to be warm.
Read this picture first. Then,
if you can, prefer the lies again.

> In truth, diggers recover and grow
> such gardens so lovingly laboured over.

from Going and Coming

2: The Bog-Oak Dragons

for Jo Habib, who was there

Cwm Nantcol: cutting peat from the bog,
time upon Time turned up a pickled
limb or stump of oak, black log
on the way to coal, dark near-glitter
on the way to a lad's pocketknife whittling.

'Why always dragons?' we asked of one
of the lads, now nonagenarian -

this dragon his. (Another's was hung
at Plas Blaendol. You find them in junkshops;
one - dart-stabbed? Wormy? - salooned
in a pub). 'Why not, say, celtic crosses?'

'Easy', he answered. 'them oatmeal sacks
had a dragon for a logo, big black

bugger. Fit him to each lad's lump
of bog-oak, whack in her outlines with nails
for knifing in like picture-by-numbers'.
Out of industry, then, not Wales?

'Noson Lawen', he murmured: 'girls singing,
lads at the back can't just be sitting'.

Later: 'it's having a place in a thing'.
Old eyes close, old fingers gnarl
and itch - to be whittling again, d'you think,
in a warm time of lads and darling
lasses? The past looks wary, but winks.

3: Clown

for Alan Powers

Bumpkin, Hodge, Clown, they called
those knockabout commoner lads with the lumpen
games and the odder play-names: Bold
Slasher, Blatherdick, Hub Bub Hump-and-Scrump
Hopper Joe, Squarson, Big Head'n' Little Wits,
Esum Esquesum, Tenpenny Nit.

Kill, then put new life in place,
went the plots. Slapsticks abundant for the thwack
that did it. Mudface, blackface, paintface,
rosettes, patches on front and back,
and the world was changed. Bumpkin's cry
on entry, *In Comes I* -

'til in came city, factory, mill
with other wha's'names from a different patch
and Transformations a thing to watch,
not to do. Pay at a theatre's till
for weirdos and harlequins. Time not a season
but a clock, and commonsense unreason.

Ha! In comes no-name, paintface, bits
patched on him rosettes, bagsful of tricks,
slapsticks, Pantaloon's pomp to knock down.
No harvest, true but commonsense plain
and... Bloody Norah! they're calling him Clown!!!
It's pantomime. *Here We Are Again.*

4: Three Prentice Pieces

In the car-boot sale, a wooden pulpit,
large doll's house size, even the silliest
detail exact. 'Load of bullshit'
says a glancer-by. But a stander-still
'That's prentice work. Man, it's brilliant'.

*

Sixty years back and you could watch
the master builders' apprentice pass-outs:
young lads quarter-scaling, from a batch
of blueprints, risers, half-landing, next
three risers, all banisters, rails,
newel; and gawp at youth so expert.
Then the event went missing. Masters
saw no need of the skills, blind bastards.

*

Here's an eight-sided box: seven
by seven, the height built up on fourteen
square-cut half-inch pieces, uneven
in length but once in each the important
octagon angle. Abutments a miracle,
tighter than the blocking on the pyramids!
And glows for the old man now, in this dusk
of skilling, belief, programme, just
those reds-with-darknesses mahogany musters
from love. A keepsake, a tower, a keep
on history's motte. While the people sleep.

5: The Hirwaun and Trenforest Steelworker Portraits, c 1835

Some things he painted boldly at once:
status, the friggerish buttons for instance -
John Bryant, foreman, has twenty-four,
John Cwmbran only four. Degrees
of danger also.
                One of the two
called Davies, a cinder filler, is shovelling
fire, the other has lost an eye,
Evan Bryant an arm, Thomas
Bryant, miner, has dynamite sticks
at his shoulder.
                Ten of the sixteen, look you,
look this oddsod, the painter, straight
in the eye, puzzled or challenging:
Why are you there, and we here?
With quick economy each face differs.
Familiar, for he is one of them.

We know him now as W.J. Chapman
(wouldn't you just? The name means pedlar).

He 'took', and started getting commissions,
became itinerant, ended in London -
never much good, except at details
like buttons or eyes for staring you straight
in the eye, the tree his easel was cut
from rootless of course like a man and work
photography will supersede.

7: The Last Wakes Week Train, Rhyl, 1970s

And Tracey? the plump one shouts,
nursing her baba, shielding the other
two. Ibiza by all accounts,
someone shouts back. The fond mother
shrugs:That's four then - all them Blounts
on one of the Costas, Hills and Hardys
gone to the Ballywhatsits.
      (Can't
hear much, for more now join the party,
next-but-three neighbours down Clackpatten Street).
Old Fred keeps knitting, a grandson whittles
wood with Co-op bag on the seat
for shavings.
     Numbers are more than a little
down this year. Another defeated
mill has shut, though Hardys, Hills,
Blounts seem to be finding life sweet
enough. And Tracey?
      Staying in Rhyl
again? they ask. Our Katy's Pete
thought try the new one Wha's'name advised.
Should be ashamed of herself, that Liz.

A knitter, a whittler…Not running late!
Nan's budging, cheeks like a peach
with excitement. We've stopped. She'll get in a tizz
with that bag of patchwork to do on a beachful
of Frisbees. Hand her down easy, mate.

8: PJ de Loutherbourg, 1740-1812, arr. London '71

for David Phillips

Sometimes you need the outsider's view,
one less stuck in the local than you,
and PJ de Loutherbourg will do

nicely. Professional painter, newcomer,
picks up the facts quite early. *Midsummer
Afternoon with Methodist preacher,* a stunner

of a commonland scene of '77:
the well-to-do, the skint-as-the-devil
and the needle's eye between hell and heaven.

Then, 1800, *Coalbrookdale
by Night* - and profit's whole
red hellmouth of a country turning industrial.

Between great paintings, to Drury Lane
for Garrick, later for Sheridan,
he works at stage-sets, on illusion

not on reality, on panto
and opera. Known as de Lanternbourg
backstage, for his machine-age antics

with light. He is what's discovered -
new works, new labour, new art - ironbridges over
frig-arts gone undercover

while Time bangs on. Has fashion's approval
for his *Eidophusikon*, that groovy
introduction to the movies.

The Bishop's Prologue

The play's topography and class divisions established. THE BISHOP, much practised in this ecclesiastical art, opens the show cold. He is happy to do so, the rhymes, tumbling out like potatoes from the inexhaustible sack of his mind.

Good friends, you are to visit the city
of Bindil. I have (I think) as pretty
a knowledge of it as even the shortest-winded local vicar,
and am here to impart it semi-officially and quicker.
First, we are much like you. (Indeed, in convocation
the other Bishops and I all felt that Bindil did very well
                    for the whole nation.
For example, many locally feel compelled to seek
a new Industry, since another of ours went bust last week)

Our compact but thriving Business Area
runs from the War Memorial, here, to this our all-electric, if
                    rather shabby, Cleanliness-next-to-
                    Godliness Washetaria.
There, to the north, are Residences;
here Dwellings. There, Dwellings. There, more Dwellings.
                    The fences
of Lord Libdin's land run so:
(He is in some roundabout way related to our Queen, you
know, and many of us hope will now put up a stake
for a new Factory). Here, to the Glory of God and for His
                    Sake,
my own modest Cathedral. We are also proud
of this, our common, always to be left unploughed -
though furrowed deep each night in Sin
committed in the bushes it is abounding in.

Over there, guarding one bush, is the secretary of the Young
                    Communist League, Charles Quinn.
Of course, the wickedness here is of a low-class sort,
the better-off being far less easily caught

(though they are just as full of sin, for them it is
done to commit it on private premises
and even - since generally we keep up-to-date - with girls
                          called in by telephone.)

Adjoining the common - and Bindil is alone,
I'm sure, in this - are not the usual rented allotments, but
                          Private Plots the owners leave quite wild
in happy contrast to how they are domiciled.

That man, for instance, dragging planks towards that trunk,
is the Assistant Manager of our principal Bank, James Monke.
The tree is on his plot. (It is presumptuous in Man,
even in Bishops, to foretell God's Plan.
But Bindil is, as I've said, an average spot
and Assistant Bank Managers are the kind of hero we have
                          usually got).

Now I must go - for this is about the o'clock
that bushes most attract what is now the increasing number of
                          unemployed among my flock.
So. Like you (or you wouldn't be here) we like an evening
                          out and a bit of bonhomie.
Just the same, we are all of us up here just as worried as any
                          of you out there by both the local
                          and the National Economy.

Song before Embarkation, 1943

Tell me when I climb the side
And watch this island lumbering west
Why old Europe has to die
Before there's peace, loving at last.

Tell me when I drop this pack,
Barged among the kitbag men
With rifled laps where children sat,
Tell me when I take the bren

And run the beaches crossed with fire
And hunker down into a ditch -
Tales of Decency's and the Poor's
black enemy, Privilege.

Tell me the moral of these tales:
What gentleness must leave for dead
(Even becoming what it kills);
That lurch of heart and loss of head

Alone bring blacknesses to doom.
Tell me now. Dug-out is all
The time peace has - this grave room
In a mean while - available.

Incident in Training

lines inflated from a small news item,

We will proceed, the Sergeant said,
from General to Particular.
The cause is just. Right. Hazzuah!
Stab at that dummy of straw 'til it's quite dead.

The chaplain, too, to the same uneasy
Private: look, he argues kindly,
we do not ask you to go in blindly.
Only believe, as in prayer, while you give at the knees.

But the particular Private would
continue to see things another way.
He was to stab and pray - not they -
for faith. And then, praise God, he understood.

I'm a Particular, he cried;
but the dummy, snatching his bayonet,
struck back. There's been no bulletin yet
Mourning because some homogenous General died.

Calendar Song

The apples I ate in Bedfordshire
    mocked me with red from Alamein
and yellow from sand and the sun that's there
    and green from the wounds in Englishmen.

The leaves that tumbled on Somerset
    like parachutists from a war
brushed down my khaki battle-suit
    shaming my millions everywhere.

The big bare trees in St. James's Park
    stretched out their arms like camouflage
and ducks came down like Sunderlands
    and kids pushed off in a landing barge.

I lay by daffodils in Kent
    while men in steel drove up the sky
to toss the earth at an enemy point
    and my colonel said leisurely, by and by.

But o, when they woke me up in June
    and told all thumbs to touch the news
I heard my boats grind into France
    and the prisoning seasons let me loose.

'Then, by inspiration, I threw overboard all the plums' - Joshua Slocum, off the Azores, poisoned by a meal of plums and cheese

We take the rations in the natives give,
both cheese and plums; and then, on the high seas,
must die and have to be inspired to live.

It might so easily have been the cheese
that scuppered *Sailing Alone Around the World*
'til the words ran under salt tears, 'til a breeze

skipped over Slocum's grave, 'til we unfurled
our sails to sail alone again. But the plums
went overboard instead; the water purled

like the book, which is a pearl. And so it comes
perhaps - the inspiration comes - or not,
since all we put in belly or book or dumbshow

(when we are stuck for words?) is only what
was there in the cabin'd stores. The crew a single
hand, the cured by guess, we can be hot

or cold as a blind man's buff, buried in shingle
or off alone about the world - who write
who eat and drink or jettison words, who mingle

one with another sense, who take and bite
on what seemed wholesome to the native appetite.

Late Bermudas

Who live on islands circumscribe themselves
with sea, and all we are is all the land
there is behind frontiers of rock and sand.

This is the world. Height is the mountains here
however small, depth these declivities,
distance the patchwork haze an Englishman sees

over lazing crops. Totems are church steeples,
taboos chapels, pleasures the nearby ricks,
wildflowers one thousand four hundred and eighty-six.

Colours are Indies-hot and extravagant
that runs most riot on cold apples where, too,
the taste varies, the texture, the orchard view.

Who live on islands insulate themselves.
A thin green wire earths us to native dirt
and a black and red nonplus and plus and avert

the shock of history on hope in us.
Black is the cock castle on its rock midden
slithering down about villages poorly hidden;

black is the sludge and shale plunging to dreg
new depths by every slate and coal quarry;
black is the minus colour and the word sorry,

The plus is red and floats new islands up -
for, being insular, we cannot add
save in the terms of what we have always had

or so it seems. Arthur is rowed to another
island - Utopia perhaps, or Prospero's
isle, or the Isle of Pines, even the gloss

Marvell put upon marvellous new Bermudas.
Workaday ebbs like breakers to leave a foot
imprinting Friday on the shores of Lilliput.

Behind the tumblehomes of rock and sand,
who live on islands press or are volunteered
to the black will of mad captains, and the weird

and wonderful English written (so it is read)
of green pastures at eventual peace. If yes,
no man is an island and continents are the less

for the loss of him, why, only an islander
would think of that. And the second Republic we bore
floated, electric, off Spithead and the Nore.

So we respond to islands, hot and remote
or cold and close as dead sailors on the shore.

Preparing for Bed after Reading Pope

Tugging my socks off, it's the metre
that gets me - not the overtones
in the name (to a quaker like me) of Peter,
Paul, sin now and make no bones
of it later.
        Here are two bare feet.
Four is a more attractive number.
Five? The acerbities come sweet
and modern: I see why Byron rumbled
away in the praise of this Pope only.
But why pentameters? A live
dimension missing? God, but I'm lonely.

Heroic couplets? Five and five
make ten; but what can you do with ten?
Or were they truly heroic? Had
they something about them beyond mere men -
apart, that is, from women?
                              Mad
bastards this that invented trouser-zips.
My foreskin's caught? Ouch! Shimmy them over the hips.
Now there's a heroic couplet! My rhymes
more often go by quadruped
among the beasts that stalk our times.
Christ, I could do with a girl's feet in my bed.

Snow in the Early Morning at Putney

The snow has rendered flat and clean
as paper such dimensions as cars
have, or parked bushes, and the green
shadows on green that heighten grass.
So white, that nothing shadows nothing,
the milk-float's track marks like a crease
that topmost sheet that only scuffing
allows cold fingers to release.
The square-paned windows offer me
stacked cartons of stationery.

Only the Thames runs black, unspools
a tide of ribbon between the here
of Putney and far Fulham, where gulls
mark space and starlings group in words
like a finished sentence tapped on to straight
neighbourly roods. The black in sight
is just that twitching inch with a gate
at centre. Buildings to left and right,
neat as a typewriter's top panel,
cover the Cotswolds and the channel.

Later, day will mark the sheet:
birds, flapping, come late to school
with notes scribbled by pencil feet,
or a schoolboy smudge down a side-rule,
or a cat like a black blot squat
with its trembling edges. Or sudden thaw
prickle the whole of the paper hot
in a rash of sense, laid there before
but overlaid. Or another fall
be like another page to scrawl.

I know nothing to compare
with thus opening the curtains on air
filled with such possibility-
save white packets, black ribbon,

machine - my trade - and myself to decree
what weather shall happen out of his nibs,
my fingers. If I wish for success, it is for some such littleness
as making the pattern of snow's surprise
men wake with delight to recognise.

Another Four Characters

1: Tripper, Harlech

People will come for miles to see a ruin
clinking at turnstiles or dodging furtive past keep
and the daft sheep as crooks or kids, hallooing
from battlement, saying Caw. Jackdaws leap
outraged over dank oubliettes the desperate screw in.

Why people come for miles is the curious matter.
Is it the Past inspires us with a dead achievement?
Or pride in what can seem common bereavement?
Awed silences punctuate the chatter.

Good at detecting fakes, we are angered should
the fabric present new patches making good
the Past in terms of Now - as if they could!

A stranger's heartbroke look, arrowslit, on the bus
home excites no Caws, has no effect on us.

2: Girl in a Yellow Sack

Always in fashion, seldom at a loss
for phrase or the accessories of dress,
often some outrage makes her exceedingly cross
and war-rumours cause her acute distress.

Her manner charming, all her talk sincere
the human instincts seem almost intact
and when her friends address her as 'my dear'
it is in supposition of this fact.

The bomb appals her - so she says with passion
standing quite frightened in a yellow sack.
The party's ruined. She'll go home to bed.

But surely Sunday night will bring her back
unchanged, still yellow, out of human fashion
with no accessory ashes on her head.

3: Church Dignitary

The legend abounds in fish. Denominations
swish from the gunwales of God's anointed trawler
netting for shoals, potting the odd crawler.
Missionaries harpoon from the bluewhale stations.

The catch in, conscience flaps for its element
of sin, each eye stain-glass-glazed. Then the guts
are drawn. Poor rich, you're saved. Back to their huts
these dog-necked fishermen can sail content.

Back to great barns built for the cure to follow.
Gunners are haddock with the lust smoked out,
soused sergeants call out filleted night patrols,

generals get kippered. But into the trembling hallow
of our tiny peace there bawls that trawling lout
Archbishop Fisher - from his cure of couls.

4: Commuter

Conclusions, our destination along lines laid
ahead, narrow. The future constantly recedes
as we approach, and the present becomes frayed
in a blur of milestones, foliage and altering speeds.
Entrained with us, should he be undismayed?

Here in the compartment fellow travellers
lift up opposite dailies against the hint
that they are anyone's fellow except as the print
ties a date on all crossword unravellers.

Steam smacks on the window on wet leaf.
Fellows had made believe with him, and no thief
can remove it. So he is left alone with that belief.

Conclusions sharpen to bayonet-point as we halt
for the tunnel. If it is his fault, it is our fault.

The Loss of View from Hafodty

for Edward and Dottie Thompson

Now that difficult forests grow
where local farming failed,
no downview opens, no
far-fetched widespread world.

Only at corners of a hacked track
for the machines to ride
are squints possible, leper-like
but out from shut inside.

Darkening politics aspire
narrow as conifers
or chapel hymns - except the choir
is bogey, spook, all-fours.

The truth is Opposite is true.
Black is for sky by night,
and yet at underfoot, by the tree-
root, is most lack-light.

All predictable movement rubs
close to noiselessness
as prayer, and old intention stubs
his toe on once-wall, less-

than-wall. Trees as prison bars
update a garbled fence.
Hobble on by the guide stars
Memory, Impenitence.

Flask

The vacuous grin is that curved bowl, the mask
wrapping experiment in a vacuum flask.

All reasonable air we breathe is out
with sense and thought and certainty and doubt

and a pupil sees, reflected as he observes,
his own straight learning look twitched up by curves.

If the grin should slip, why pressure is bearing in
and lips twist down the mouth upon that skin

'til the whole pit crumples into a heap for scrap.
Instead of standing among us is a gap.

But often experiment works and the man still grins:
a happier outcome for us, who give two pins

and properly study Man, but rarely study
the actual emptiness in anybody.

Assume, if we must, a space that was once human
kind to bodies both politic and woman

that now is void. And we may even guess
at no collapse, at a drowned lung's long distress.

But while that newly emptied space reflects
and tips up the lips to pleasure, England expects

and Nature need not abhor what we permit.
O have no fear. Self-pity will sump that pit.

Lines on a Ladies Magazine Feature for the 50th Anniversary of World War I

In fifty years see how the green grass
and barbed bramble have taken over
from helmet and boot and skull and cross
as frame or under Nature's hegemony, as cover.

Our editorial habit with any art
is to abstract, as here from poets, the lament
and picture this bodymatter well set out
between columns of advertisement.

So here we are able with fine photographs
to mark proof and put to bed
by Thomas and Owen, Sassoon and Graves
this timely and well-supported doublespread.

This morning's whiff of news from the Yemeni
comes from the stink of a daily paper.
Within our covers war comes under the hegemony
of all the advertised perfumes of Arabia.

Bee Notions

214. The Sting of a Bee. 657. Apply honey.
(John Wesley, *Primitive Physic*, 1747)

They buzz as the brains of people buzz.
They sting sometimes. Apart from the Queen
(and who cares about her?) they build

by a science near geodesics.
Raw materials they glean
without spoil from rose, late daffodil,

all wildflowers: free. Bee industry
is much admired by such as write
Utopias (though the lack of leisure

keeps it away from mine). And yet
what they make is rich as milk, and quite
remarkably useful, however you measure

out differences. Wesley advises
a dressing of onions and then of honey
as a cure for baldness; the British Mead

Association deals with rising
damp (granted both time and money)
by adding honey to the plaster screed.

(Better waste in than out, say I:
mead is potent, let the walls trickle).
Nor ever are honeys the same thing twice:

on Crete spicy with herbs, Fortnums
sell them godknows-flavoured - to tickle
the jaded rich, judging by price.

Others, less privileged, once rough-musicked
passing swarms: come down, me dears,
and hive in this poor settlement.

And then, eventually. folk die.
One ancient commoner's custom steers
the bees even to that event -

to be propitiated this:
'John Gee is dead, and his son is master,
who sends you something from each dish

and jug on the table. We hope you'll be
content with him as new master' -
in those days still a sensible wish.

But busy as bees, a people's brain
looks at the business, does a sum,
finds Capital now, on its own terms, bust

far beyond anyone's honeyed words.
'John Greed is bankrupt. Commonwealth come!'
Milk and honey for the lot of us!

Chapter Four

from a discontinued 1980s verse novel

Ticket? He cannot find his ticket. Kindly the inspector
    smiles,
So he smiles back, putting a hand in his other jacket
    pocket.
Lurching about as the train buckets and swings through
    indifferent miles
Of England, the hand closes - on what? Ah yes. (He thinks
    of his son
And blushes slightly.) Behind the inspector and himself
    a nation piles -
Bound for refreshment perhaps or, as a consequence, any
    toilet
Unoccupied, and a honeymoon couple who've sped down far
    more aisles
Than they had bargained for, dainty fingers afire round
    plastic teacups.
Try the compartment? the inspector asks, well up to most
    men's wiles,
And slides a door to suit the words. Confused, he follows
    in.
A stout lady, one of the kind that appears in agglomerate
    styles
Of uniform, clearly regards him as under arrest and
    gulps;
A smart banker frowns up from an imposing lapful of
    files.
The wrong compartment? suggests the inspector gently,
    easing him out.
He cannot remember. They try two or more of these
    pigeonhole domiciles
Before he can settle at home. But still he fails to produce
    a ticket.

*

Out of the corridor he can at last explore back pockets,
    tight
Though they are in a fashion current for the middle-aged.
    His hand first jams
And then bursts forth with a snap of Bella and the kids
    by flash-light.
An almost identical stout lady in the corner nods in
    approval.
Yours? she asks: so little stability these days, but *they*
    look bright
(Meaning the kids, he supposes, those adolescent terrors.)
    The suit
Is new and strange to him still, with no left pocket at the
    back; but quite
The thing, they'd said. Fumbling his bum like a fool, Eh?
    he says, startled.
Someone has asked his destination. Eh? An. Well. For
    tonight
Oswestry, then Chester. Sort of a tour. My office or
    wife
Must have muddled things up in my briefcase: a tour from
    site to site.
The almost identical banker doesn't think much of this.
    (Neither
Does he, who can't stand chatterers.) The inspector, too
    has a slight
They're-not-so-often-so-stupid look. Oswestry? Beeching
    cut
That out, oh years ago, All Right! he shouts. Gobowen,
    then. Right?
On the other line! (They've cut all sense from lines
    and meaning and place.)

    *

He snatches his unscratched, brand-new briefcase down from
    the luggage-rack,
Unzips it, flings the lid. Search that! he cries; and the
    stout lady
Lets out a screech and a long hiss, as if for a tunnel's
    black,

And drags from her handbag a Bible. The banker tut-tuts
　　　to the lap of files.
For it's all there, this life, as exposed as a naked man on
　　　his back:
The cut-off notice from Manweb, pyjamas soused from a
　　　fountain pen spill,
The tube of ointment for piles, Bella's enormous
　　　'Remember to pack
Your razor', no razor, the sexy underpants purchased to
　　　turn her on,
Timothy Lea's *Confessions of a Window Cleaner*, a plastic
　　　map -
The stout lady has turned, by accident or design, to
　　　Revelations -
The school report that so worries Bella and him about young
　　　Jack.
Seeing all this, he shouts No! It's not all there. There's
　　　this and this
And this! An he empties on to the heap - smack, smack,
　　　smack -
The contents of all his pockets. With such great violence
　　　does he move
That the condoms his hand had closed on earlier burst out
　　　of their pack -
Out - everywhere - as if from all his pockets - his ticket
　　　among them.

*

The inspector goes at last. No, he will not grin and
　　　explain.
The stout lady, who is gently puffing now on some up-
　　　gradient
Of soul, searching for lost stability, must therefore
　　　remain
In ignorance of the fact that *Confessions of a Window
　　　Cleaner*
Is merely its covers wrapped round a devotional work on
　　　the nature of Pain.
(He had not wished his office colleagues to think him the
　　　prig he may be.)

And the banker, who had budged an inch, may well have
    piles himself,
A common desk-bound hazard. And he can easily think of
    a stain
Far worse than ink on a pair of pyjamas, And who on earth
    pays Manweb
Before the cut-off notice? And - going back a bit - how
    daft to strain
Your bladder with tea on the way to whatever sort
    of honeymoon
You intend. Oh God, young Jack and the nextdoor neighbour's
    nubile Jane!
Surely the world understands? That look in the eye, that
    hand in pocket,
And the early age at which all young bucks these days
    entertain
Designs on neighbourhood daughters. A father's duty to
    provide is plain.
He stuffs them back in their pack, and laughs, and later
    laughs again.

*

Opens the paper. War described as Defence! It's all
    pretence
Save Bella. Looks up: why read the stuff? Outside, a
    scene's cut off
As soon as focused. Par for the course, then: destinations
    from stations,
Relations - who knows? - with neighbours, manwebs, covers
    from content, lovers
Often alas, bankers from fashion. All that is left
    to do,
England out there, is giggle or weep, but find one other
    to be true to.

Sunday in August 1968

Under their sloppy hats the girls
Dangle like magnified flowers on grass:
Harebells, Canterbury bells,
convolvulus; and the young men pass

Admiringly as nature-lovers.
Windstreams have slunk mile off today,
No aircraft split the sky above us
And no cars farting on the motorway

Are a pollution we forgot.
Here is peace, and the girls play cool
And young, and the young men young and hot.
Sound lets fall its petals on a pool

Of green. Nothing, it seems, can spoil
Or pollute or deafen a day like this:
The seventh after six of toil,
Nature in a parenthesis

Within the sentence of our work.
But the brackets close. Into this modern
Peace the church bells bang, jerking
At naturalness. And the word of God

Batters its hideous din on the brain,
splitting the sky and reason. No
Lovers petition or complain.
The mutations happened generations ago

And we are monsters deformed by Jesu's
raucous church if this is peace.

Calculated Acts

If love is all, privacies add
to what's assessed as the proper rate
of tax on working lass and lad:
        what sum from what they make.

And if the tax is put to work
by government for some greater good
then lovers read, when they awake,
        a budget in the news.

Can this be us? they ask of it
watching the way their passions go
to balancing a deficit
        of hate for some great foe,

and turn in bed, to improve the sum
if love is all. But take a chance
on beggary in bodies come,
        like dust, to impotence.

Or leave the bed for a short while
to offer politics a nudge
towards bankruptcy for hate. Not all,
        alas, but love is much.

Waiting for the Revolution by Siop Parry

The mother asks, 'Anything coming?
Either way?' Her son
looks right for 'No', and left for 'No',
then is let run

arriving just as myself must cross.
But had preferred (I guess)
to get here quicker than wait on machinery's
readiness.

Down the hill I look to a past
where I have often been,
and up to the brow where what might come
cannot be seen.

Neither looks for an accident.
Child (he thinks) for years,
and I for years, have hoped against hope
and against fears.

The Migneint, with an Image of Christ

This is that wilderness where Christ
sat by the devil's easel; and does
tempt. Wool nuzzles the diamond lakes
and plains are rich as chessboards diced
in marquetry. Rivers buzz
and loop to a honey sea that makes

for islands odd as the cloud we're under.
His elevation must have showed
to Him images now shown us
and, in his more than month of Sundays,
narrowing mind and eye have slowed
to a choice less than impetuous.

Knight and bishop sidestep and boss
on ruly courses. Pawns like ants
budge from one slated square to the patient
blank of work, then to black doss
again - though, to be sure, a chance
exists of endboard coronation

here, where the peak-caps tipped and winked
for Tudors. Cock castle crow
on royal middens. Villages press
to the ground. Men go. Blue-black-inked
the dead quarries spread and flow
to hook like squid on nakedness.

History's evidence of hate
and greed is here impartial as lichen.
Each time has tombs to mark the offence.
And Christ, refusing to be great
by wealth, presents an image less rich in
sanctity than profound common sense.

Ysbyty Goffa

to Huw Jones, my GP who attended me there; to Valmi Roberts, my neighbour, an ex-nurse; and in memory of my old friend the architect Clough Williams-Ellis who designed the place.

I

Four of us, old men: the first
unable to speak , the second to stop speaking
(my nextbed neighbour, a joker whose grafts have
               come undone),
the third with self- or wife-inflicted burns
he'll not explain, while I,
breathless, snort on a thing like a shell left over
               from World War One.

Blue patches in a shadow-white sky,
nurses arrive on business, this time banging
pillows, changing the sheets. Bedding take wing,
               go flapping
up in the shapes of gulls, and seem to fly,
gossip, cackle too,
funny about the neighbours, rumours that this or that
               has happened.

More colours. Green for cleaners, mud-
brown for a doctor, and is it white for food?
But more kaleidoscopic sightings : vision jiggle and
               shake.
Visitors, but whose? Like shadows a-scud
on a hillside, near-far things,
everyone's relative: nurse, visitor, him dying,
               us: half-awake.

Here the world's a common weather to
us all. No single visitor speaks to the one
bed only. We are encouraged, to walk
               make sense, do.

Nextbed and I move drunkenly together
along the Ward to its Day Room,
daylight, a wall of windows, Wales, immensity,
                the outside view.

II

Viewpoints hang in the air above
Cwm Bowydd, Blaenau's secret, a palm
whose fingers lift (on the left)
                to the sprawled estate
of town and country, and (on the right) shove
us, thumb us back up the *Moelwyns*,
The Manods, to home, danger, history's trademark
                spoilheaps of Slate.

Before us, light unmuffles distance
little by little. The *Bowydd* wanders and falls
to an unseen lower shelf, then down
                to a lower still,
further and further down to *Cymerau isaf*
past *Plas Dolmoch* until
Traeth Bach sails history off and high seas
                makes the only hill.

You can guess those invisible shelves, detect
them only by what they hoist into sight,
ranges of oyster, elephant and smoke-grey
                mountainscape,
loom after loom. Were you an architect
you'd assume the Plan and these
would be Elevation, sections built up by footwork
                and measuring tape.

But being sick forgets profession.
Senses are all. The mountains tremble in sun
the slate behind us, Rhinogs
                and even further before -
each with its little secret possession
a *Bowydd*, a *Teigl*, a *Cynfal*
to grow and quarrel and marry and swell to the *Traeth*
                which the legends fought for.

Curtains of distant rain draw back
to show an even greater distance, and a weird
backcloth, Cader even. Every foisted slope
                a theatrical flat ;
passing squalls an attack
of actors in flaring cloak like
clouds. Great actors stirring legends as health
                stirs hope.

III

No Welsh chorister but songster
for all that - nextbed says he's off to sing
the Women's Ward goodnight. Nursing his grafts,
                he has to shuffle
past single wards and offices,
a long veranda,
all facing, as main wards do, that distance,
                that permanence, that past.

The town and recent history
is at our backs, the other side of the passage
nextbed walks, unseen, taken for granted ;
                out-patients'
waiting room, unseen kitchens ; industry
(or its remains) beyond ;
shops, homes, school, buses and trains
                give us a shout.

Clear and white everything looks
as health improves, with a black trim everywhere.
Clough built the place in the twenties
                as a memorial
To the dead slaughtered beside him, and as harbour.
Even his architect's drawings,
in these days much forgotten, have their trim
                of a black border.

All this looking into the distance
is his therefore. The cliff-edge perch
for take-off. Immediate pasts behind one's
                shoulder.
At this time too, behind another contour,
Another hoist of his, Portmeirion…

Nextbed's sense of our situation
differs from mine. Well soldiers yes, he says,
but also the quarrymen. Never forget the bloody
                slate.
The union took a penny off the pay
to fund the work, he says,
and chaps put in free building time to keep
                things up to date.

IV

Recovering now, we sit up late
looking out at the older worlds of Wales
and the setting sun, till starlight outshines
                the window lights
snapped off or curtained in where the beds wait.
Only occasional headlamps
probe then die, like an usherette's torch in the
                amphitheatre of night.

But the earth has turned its half-circle
stars are glittering eyes fixed upon us.
the all-night-lights are here and the only
                action here.
We are history if history's said to be working.
We are what's left of legend.

V

'The bastards are going to shut the place'
someone comes shouting, 'And in the name of health!'
cries another. Dame Charity enters : a moment of calm :
        'They cannot mean it.'
But do. Send on a Pantomime Dame.
It's farce this; not drama.
Statistics fly past like custard pies.
        Also movement by stealth.

The bastards are going to shut the place.
That was last night's rumour. The bastards are going
to shut the place. They have consulted us, they say
and now they must shut the place. To our face
they say it, lying bastards.

Nextbed off for further treatment, the burnsman also.
I'm home in the town. The other man died.
The town is furious. Marches. Meetings.
There is after all a worthwhile drama
for the Mabinogion to watch.

Back to a town grown stiff with anger,
far beyond rumour. Stiff and fixed as the lettering
on a good slate tombstone, or the unalterable
        lines
of legend. Back with the certainties of health
to the place where people live.

A Note on the Text

Arnold Rattenbury finished putting together this collection shortly before his death in April 2007. That is to say, he left several competing MSS and TSS in various stages of correction, each with a slightly different list of contents, including poems with alternative titles, some of which appear to be either lost or unwritten. An alternative sub-title for this book might be 'unpublished, uncollected, unfinished and unwritten poems.' I have tried to follow Rattenbury's plans for the book as faithfully as is possible in the circumstances, putting the new poems at the beginning and his last poem - also unfinished - at the end.

In a hand-written note to one of the versions of this book, Rattenbury explained that 'a large part of this collection is of poems escaped (or fired) from earlier collections.' Five poems - 'Then, by inspiration', 'Late Bermudas', 'Snow in the Early Morning at Putney', 'Preparing for Bed after Reading Pope' and 'Incident in Training' - are from an untitled MS dated 1969-71. 'Bee Notions' was written in 1972 and 'Chapter Four' in 1981. 'Tripper, Harlech', 'Church Dignitary', 'Commuter', 'The Loss of View from Hafodty', 'Waiting for the Revolution by Siop Parry', 'Lines on a Ladies Magazine Feature', and 'Calculated Acts' are from an unpublished 1989 MS called 'Stepping Distance'. 'Twitching', 'Waiting with Sim', 'The Communist', 'The Bog-Oak Dragons', 'Clown', 'Three Prentice Pieces', 'The Hirwaun and Treforest Steelworker Portraits', 'The Last Wakes Week Train', 'PJ de Loutherbourg, 1740-1812,' and 'Ysbyty Goffa' are from a late, also unfinished, MS called 'Blerym, Blerym'.

'Calendar Song' was first published in *Our Time* (1944) then in *New Lyrical Ballads* (1945); 'Girl in a Yellow Sack' in the *New Reasoner* (1959). 'The Bishop's Prologue' is taken from 'The Man in the Tree: A Play of Five Acts in Doggerel', written in 1957 and performed in 1972 at the Lyceum Theatre in Crewe Theatre as *A Comedy of Good Intentions*. 'Three Prentice Pieces' was first published in *The Cambrian*

(2007) and in Andy Croft (ed) *Speaking English: Poems for John Lucas* (2007).

I am grateful to Sim and Emma for access to Arnold's papers and for helping me decipher his handwriting.

AC

Notes

Waiting with Sim
'Traeth' means a beach or shore in Welsh, here estuary.

The Communist
Evan Walters's painting 'The Communist' (1932) appears on the cover of Rattenbury's *Mr Dick's Kite* (2005).

The Bog-Oak Dragons
'Nosen Lawen' is a cheerful evening in Welsh, something like a ceilidh.

Clown
Bold Slasher, Blatherdick, Hub Bub Hump-and-Scrump, Hopper Joe, Squarson, Big Head'n' Little Wits, Esum Esquesum and Tenpenny Nit are all traditional characters in Mummer's plays. Their costume was the Mummer's shirt reproduced on the cover of this book. In his catalogue to *The Dragon, the Monster, the Fool & Other Creatures* (Salisbury, 1979), Rattenbury described this shirt as follows : 'This costume for a character in a winter Plough play - one in which a character is killed, then brought to life like Old Year/New Year - was last used in 1895 in what had then been an long unbroken tradition. The other characters, all played by men, were Tom the Fool, Recruiting Sergeant, Ribboner, Doctor, Plough-man, Threshing Blade, Farmer's Man, Dame Jane and Beelzebub. Except for Dame Jane who was a man-woman Bessy, Hopper Joe and the rest all wore the same costume of red and black figures in a white, wool-fringed smock, and all introduced themselves with the words "In Comes I". The play was funny, and very similar ones common along the Nottingham-Derbyshire border (where Cropwell Bishop is) and through Lincolnshire.'

The Loss of View from Hafodty
In note on the poem Rattenbury wrote, 'Hafodty was for long the Thompson's North Wales home, a place long known. Increasingly from the year of their expulsion from the British

communist party, the ever-thickening growth of conifer plantation around the house seriously obscured once wide and beautiful views. Perhaps it is relevant to add that Edward and I shared Methodist childhoods and board-schooling.'

Bee Notations
According to Rattenbury's notes, 'Bee Notations is a folklorist phrase for various rituals to do with bees. John Wesley's *Primitive Physic* of 1714 is organised into two numbered lists, the first of conditions prescribed for, the second of the prescriptions. Since there are many more of the latter - 5 for lunacy and 4 for Raging Madness, for instance, though only 1 each for the Bee-sting and Baldness of my poem - the two sets of numbers diverge exponentially. The ritual following John Gee's death was reported by the Rector of Sessey to the Vicar of Danby who recorded it in his *Forty Years in a Moorland Parish* of 1892.'

The Migneint, with an Image of Christ
The Migneint is a moor between Bala and Ffestiniog.

Ysbyty Goffa
Ysbyty Goffa is the name of the Community Hospital in Blaenau Ffestiniog where Rattenbury was treated for emphysema. Bowydd, Teigel and Cynfal are the names of local rivers.